TOP 10 GREAT WOMEN IN HISTORY

WOMEN IN HISTORY FOR KIDS

Children's Women Biographies

BABY PROFESSOR
EDUCATION KIDS

Speedy Publishing LLC

40 E. Main St. #1156

Newark, DE 19711

www.speedypublishing.com

Copyright 2017

History tends to be written by men, and often concentrates on what men do over what women do. However, all through history women have, as the saying goes "held up half the sky". Let's learn about ten great women in the history we all share. We'll start far back in history, and move toward the present.

HATSHEPSUT

(12TH CENTURY BCE)

Hatshepsut ruled Egypt from 1479 to 1458 BCE. She was king, or pharaoh, for over twenty years, longer than any other Egyptian woman monarch before Cleopatra.

Hatshepsut rebuilt the trade relationships between Egypt and other countries that had collapsed while Egypt was under control of the Hyksos people.

We Can Do It!

MARBLE STATUE OF HATSHEPSUT

This created a time of wealth and expansion in the country. She directed hundreds of grand pubic works projects, from roads and temples to memorials and military facilities, throughout Egypt.

She led Egypt in victorious wars to the south and east, but most of her reign was peaceful and prosperous.

TOMYRIS

(6TH CENTURY BCE)

Tomyris was the queen of a region east of the Caspian Sea in central Asia. When Persia invaded the land of her people, the Massagetae, Tomyris led her people's response. The Persians captured her son, and Tomyris challenged the Persian leader, Cyrus the Great, to a battle.

We Can Do It!

QUEEN TOMYRIS

THE HEAD OF CYRUS BROUGHT
TO QUEEN TOMYRIS

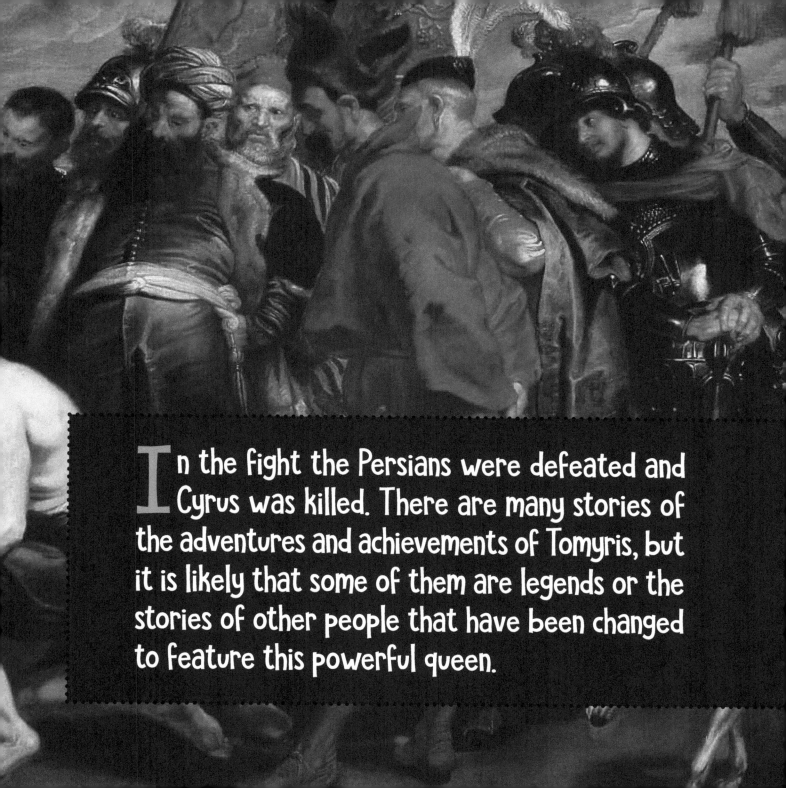

In the fight the Persians were defeated and Cyrus was killed. There are many stories of the adventures and achievements of Tomyris, but it is likely that some of them are legends or the stories of other people that have been changed to feature this powerful queen.

ARAWELO

(FIRST CENTURY CE)

Arawelo was a queen in east Africa, ruling much of the area that is now Somalia. She was the oldest daughter of the king, and fought hard for women to have the same rights as men, including the right to inherit both property and power.

We Can Do It!

Before Arawelo was queen, she organized women of her town to fetch water and help the men hunt during a long drought when the lack of rain caused a crop failure.

The men at first objected to women doing work that was not traditionally theirs, but in the end Arawelo won her way. Women did more hunting, and men started participating more in childcare and keeping the homes.

EMPRESS WU

(625–705 CE)

Empress Wu started as a concubine, brought into the emperor's house because she was very pretty and charming. She rose from that position to being the power behind the throne during the reigns of her husband and several of her children.

We Can Do It!

EMPRESS OF CHINA

She was the only female emperor in China's history, and proved to be an effective ruler. Read about her in the Baby Professor book Empress Wu: Breaking and Expanding China.

CATHERINE OF SIENA

(1347-80)

Catherine of Siena was a theologian and philosopher in Italy. Born almost the youngest of 25 children, she decided by about age seven that she wanted to join a religious order. Her parents disapproved, but she insisted, partly because this was the only way she would be able to get an education.

We Can Do It!

ST. CATHERINE OF SIENA

Catherine devoted her life to prayer, study, and service to people who were sick or poor. She took care of the sick in their homes, or in hospitals.

She campaigned for the end of the constant wars and raids between the small kingdoms of the Italian peninsula, wars that caused much misery and suffering for the poor.

On the religious front, she argued with church authorities, including the Pope, and finally convinced them of the need for reforms to the administration of the Catholic Church.

Over three hundred of her letters have survived and are some of the greatest remaining early literary works from Tuscany, her region of Italy.

Catherine was made a saint a century after her death and is highly regarded as a model for all Christians.

JOAN OF ARC

(1412–31)

Joan grew up at a time when England dominated much of France. As a teenager, she claimed to have received visions from God that she should help liberate France. Charles VII, not yet crowned king, sent her to help save the city of Orleans, which the English were attacking. Under her leadership, the French were able to force the English army away.

We Can Do It!

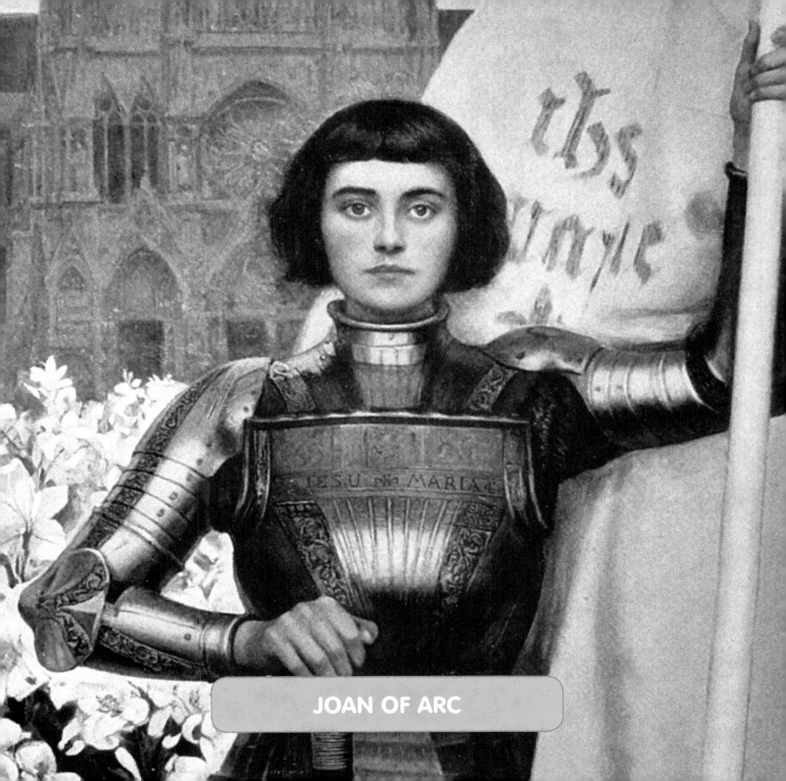

JOAN OF ARC

Joan led the French in several more victories, making it possible for Charles to be crowned king of France. She was captured by the English, put on trial for heresy (crimes against God), found guilty, and burned at the stake.

A later commission of the Roman Catholic Church found Joan innocent of any religious crime. She is considered a hero of France and was named a martyr and saint of the Church.

ELIZABETH I

(1533–1603)

Elizabeth, a daughter of King Henry VIII, ruled England for 44 years, from 1558 until her death. She was known as "The Virgin Queen" and "Gloriana", and her reign experienced great perils, and also great successes, for England. After Henry died, his young son Edward became king. When he died, Elizabeth's half-sister Mary became queen.

We Can Do It!

QUEEN ELIZABETH I

Elizabeth at this point lived in peril, as she was identified with the Protestant movement in England in opposition to Roman Catholic Mary.

GLINDONI PERFORMING AN EXPERIMENT IN FRONT OF QUEEN ELIZABETH I

She was in prison for nearly a year, and could have faced execution at any time.

However, when Mary died without having had any children, Elizabeth became queen at age 25. She was smart and well-educated, and surrounded herself with dedicated and competent administrators. Her government was able to restore the royal treasury, expand trade and England's diplomatic status in the world, and stave off a series of threats of wars and even invasions. Under Elizabeth arts, exploration, and scientific discovery flourished.

THE DEATH OF QUEEN ELIZABETH I

CATHERINE THE GREAT

CATHERINE THE GREAT

(1729–96)

Born in Poland, Catherine married Peter III, Czar of Russia. Peter was killed in an attempted coup in 1762. After order was restored, Catherine took power as the Czarina, and ruled Russia for 32 years. During her reign, Russia grew in military strength and political influence to become one of the great powers of Europe. It expanded west and south, and handed the Ottoman Empire two of its greatest military defeats in 1770.

We Can Do It!

This established Russia as the most important power in the region. Russia even planted colonies in Alaska, although later this territory was sold to the United States.

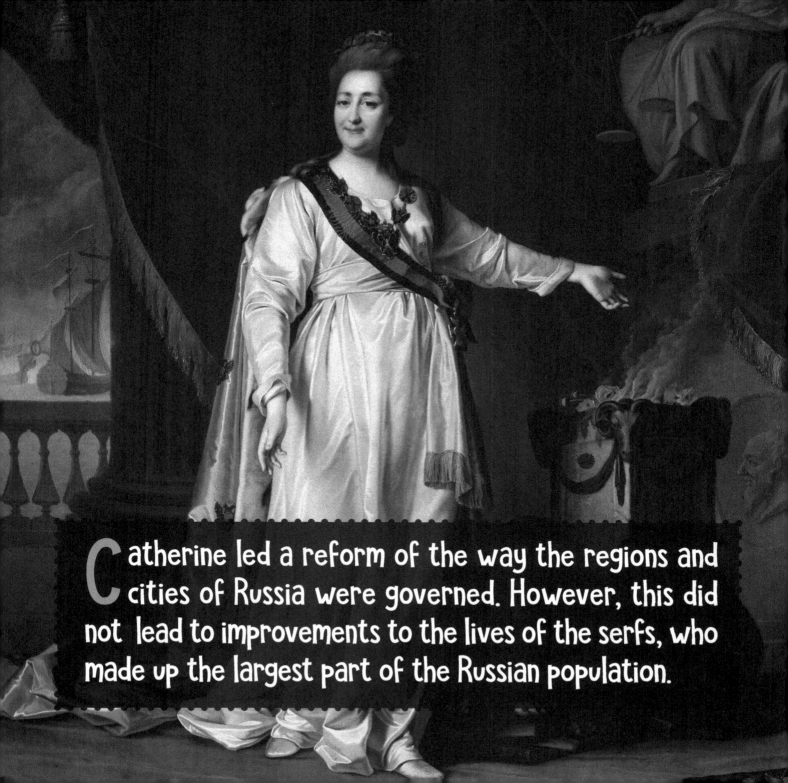

Catherine led a reform of the way the regions and cities of Russia were governed. However, this did not lead to improvements to the lives of the serfs, who made up the largest part of the Russian population.

Catherine was a patron of the arts and of learning. She helped bring enlightenment concepts in the arts and sciences to Russia from western Europe, and wanted to be thought of as a philosopher as well as a ruler. On the other hand, she acted harshly against rivals and opponents within Russia, and ruthlessly put down several rebellions during her time on the throne.

SOJOURNER TRUTH

(1797–1883)

S ojourner Truth was born as a slave in New York State in 1797. Her name at birth was Isabella Baumfree. When she escaped from slavery in 1826, she gave herself her new name. She worked to end the slave trade in the United States, to help escaping slaves, and to gain rights for both people of color and women of all colors.

We Can Do It!

SOJOURNER TRUTH

CIVIL WAR, JULY 1861

When the Civil War broke out in 1861, Sojourner Truth helped recruit African Americans to fight on the Union side against the slavery-supporting Confederate States. She had a lifelong goal of providing freed slaves grants of land and resources so they could support themselves.

Although she could neither read or write, she was a powerful campaigner for equal rights for all people.

**SOJOURNER TRUTH'S
BUST UNVEILING**

Sojourner Truth's causes included the end of slavery, prison reform, reform of property laws, and the right to vote for all people regardless of their gender or color. In her lifetime, she only saw the abolition of slavery come to pass.

FLORENCE NIGHTINGALE

FLORENCE NIGHTINGALE

(1820–1910)

Florence Nightingale, born in Italy to an English family, was a nurse, researcher, and campaigner for social reforms in the nineteenth century. She developed the standards for modern nursing and care for patients, greatly improving survival rates of patients in hospitals.

We Can Do It!

During the Crimean War, 1853-56, the British public was shocked by news reports of the horrible conditions of their wounded soldiers on the battlefields in Russia and in hospitals in Turkey. Nightingale was put in charge of nursing in the region and greatly improved sanitation, organization, patient care, and recovery rates.

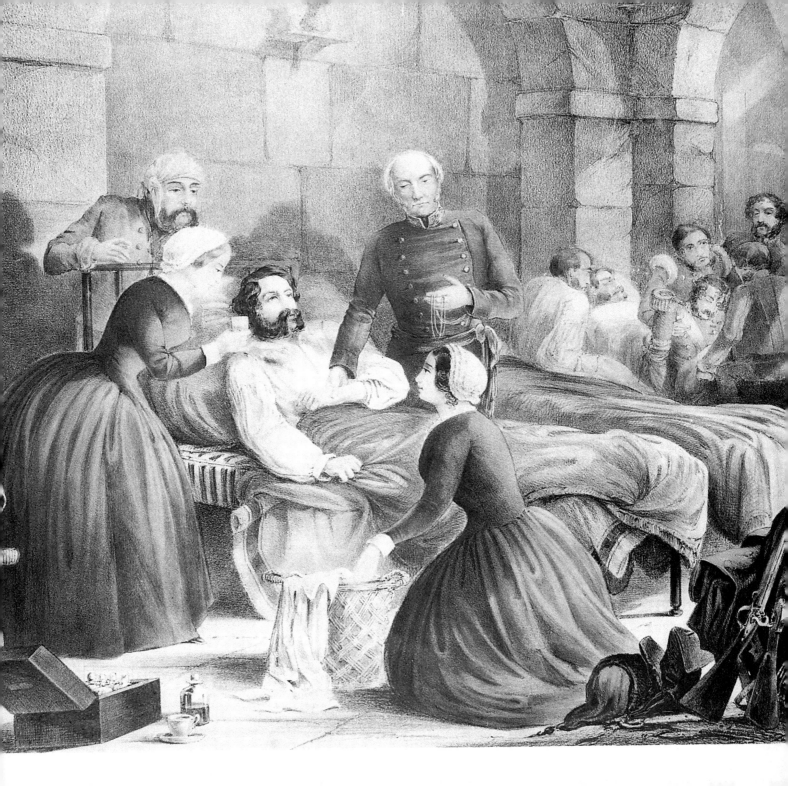

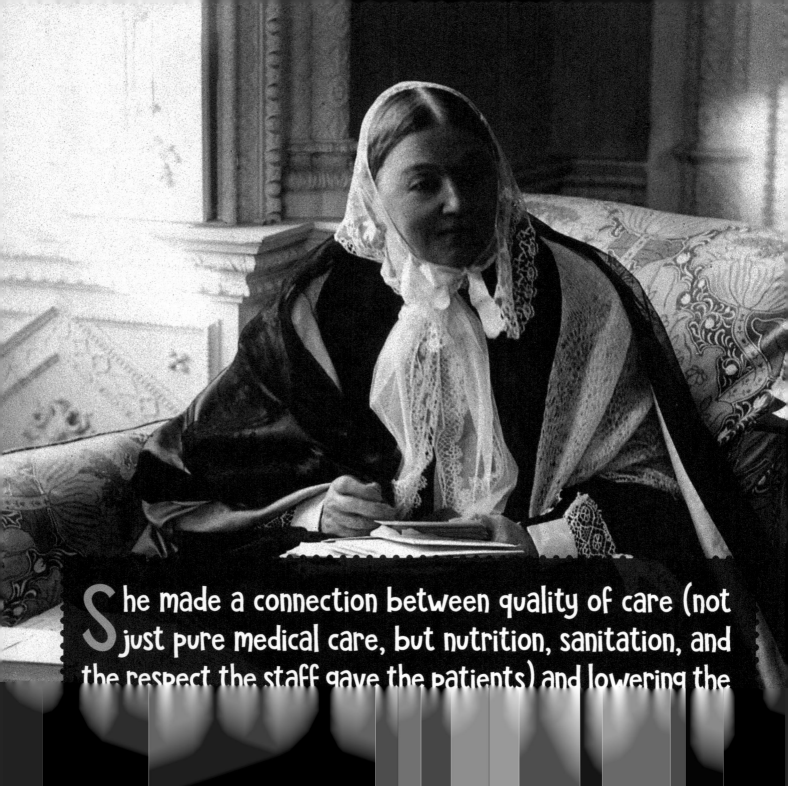

She made a connection between quality of care (not just pure medical care, but nutrition, sanitation, and the respect the staff gave the patients) and lowering the

She was known as the "lady with the lamp" for her tireless visiting with patients long into the night.

She founded the Nightingale School of Nursing to share her methods, which are the foundation of the modern practice of practical nursing, midwifery, and care for those in institutions ranging from hospitals to prisons to workhouses.

THE NEXT GREAT MAN OR WOMAN

None of these people were born great, and none of them woke up one day and decided to it was time to become great. They combined the realities of their birth and their location with hard work and commitment. You could do that, too. What will your field be?

We Can Do It!

Learn about people who found their life's work in surprising places in Baby Professor books like A Rich Man in Poor Man's Clothes: The Story of St. Francis of Assisi, Sally Ride: The First American Woman in Space, and Al Capone: A Dangerous Existence.

CPSIA information can be obtained
at www.ICGtesting.com
Printed in the USA
LVHW062146200723
753073LV00041B/1028